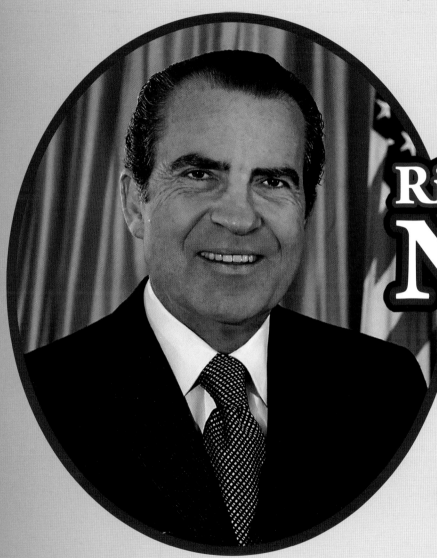

Richard M. Nixon

by Michelle M. Hasselius

Consulting Editor: Gail Saunders-Smith, PhD

Consultant:
Sheila Blackford
Librarian, Scripps Library
Managing Editor, *American President*
Miller Center, University of Virginia

CAPSTONE PRESS
a capstone imprint

Pebble Plus is published by Capstone Press,
1710 Roe Crest Drive, North Mankato, Minnesota 56003
www.capstonepub.com

Library of Congress Cataloging-in-Publication Data
Hasselius, Michelle M., 1981–
Richard M. Nixon / by Michelle M. Hasselius ; consulting editor, Gail Saunders-Smith, PhD.
pages cm. — (Pebble plus. Presidential biographies)
Includes bibliographical references and index.
Summary: "Simple text and photographs present a biography of President Richard M. Nixon"— Provided by publisher.
ISBN 978-1-4765-9612-9 (library binding)
ISBN 978-1-4765-9615-0 (paperback)
ISBN 978-1-4765-9618-1 (eBook PDF)
1. Nixon, Richard M. (Richard Milhous), 1913–1994—Juvenile literature. 2. Presidents—United States—Biography—Juvenile
literature. I. Title.
E856.H38 2014
973.924092—dc23
[B]   2013035610

Editorial Credits
Lori Bye, designer; Jo Miller, media researcher; Jennifer Walker, production specialist

Photo Credits
Corbis: Wally McNamee, 21; Getty Images: Hulton Archive, 5, Pictorial Parade, 15, Popperfoto, 9; NARA, cover, 1; Newscom:
akg-images, 13, Everett Collection, 11, 17, 19, ZUMA Press/KESTONE Pictures, 7

Note to Parents and Teachers

The Presidential Biographies set supports national history standards related to people and culture.
This book describes and illustrates the life of Richard M. Nixon. The images support early readers
in understanding the text. The repetition of words and phrases helps early readers learn new words.
This book also introduces early readers to subject-specific vocabulary words, which are defined in
the Glossary section. Early readers may need assistance to read some words and to use the Table of
Contents, Glossary, Read More, Internet Sites, and Index sections of the book.

Printed in the United States of America in North Mankato, Minnesota.
092013   007775CGS14

Table of Contents

Early Life

Richard Milhous Nixon was the 37th U.S. president. He was born January 9, 1913, in Yorba Linda, California. Richard was the second son of Francis and Hannah Nixon.

born in Yorba Linda, California

1913

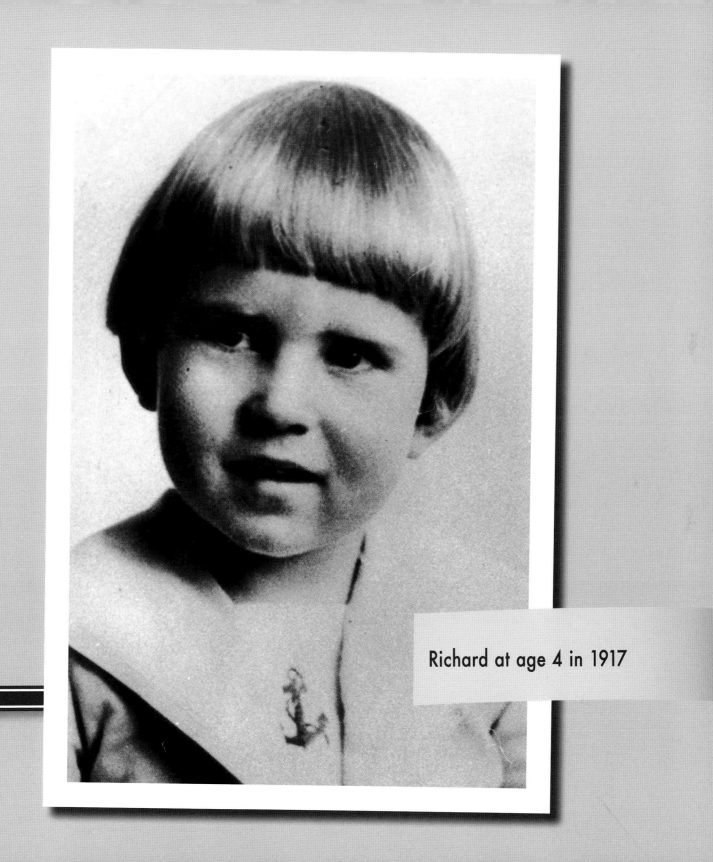

Richard at age 4 in 1917

Richard went to Whittier College after high school. Richard worked hard. He was elected student body president. In 1934 Richard went to law school at Duke University.

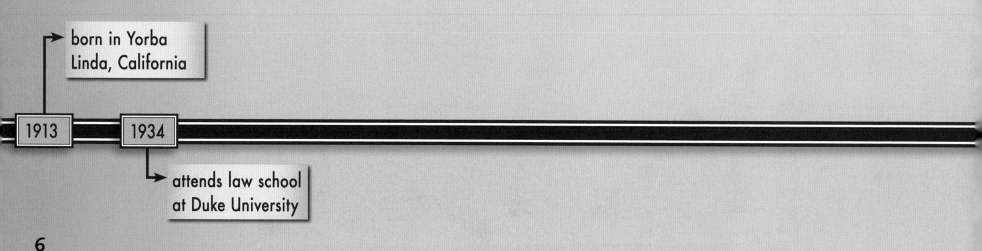

1913

born in Yorba Linda, California

1934

attends law school at Duke University

Richard (12) with his football team in the 1930s

7

Young Adult

After college Richard worked as a lawyer. One night he met a teacher named Thelma "Pat" Ryan. Richard and Pat married in 1940. They had two daughters, Patricia and Julie.

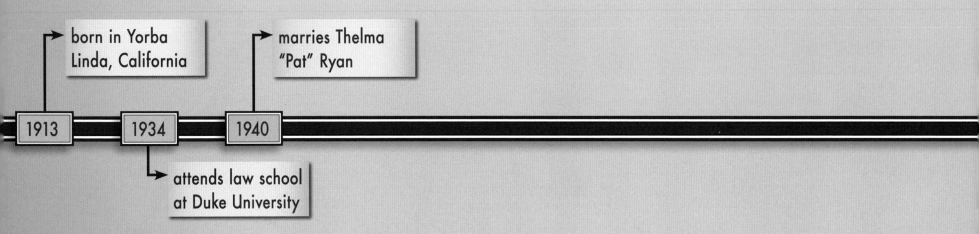

born in Yorba
Linda, California

marries Thelma
"Pat" Ryan

| 1913 | 1934 | 1940 |

attends law school
at Duke University

Richard and Pat with their daughters, Patricia and Julie, in 1950

Richard was asked to run
for U.S. Congress in 1946.
He was elected to the
U.S. House of Representatives.
Richard was elected a U.S. senator
for California four years later.

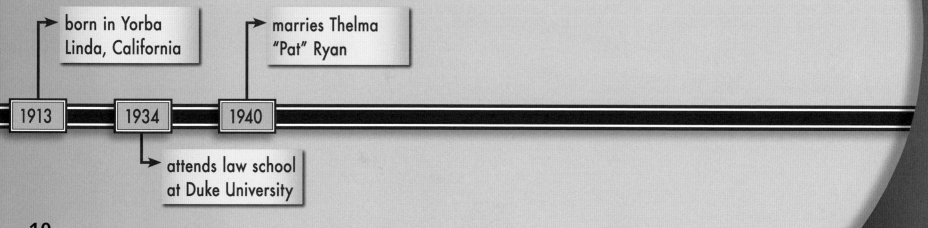

born in Yorba
Linda, California

marries Thelma
"Pat" Ryan

1913

1934

1940

attends law school
at Duke University

Richard in 1950

Life in Politics

In 1952 Richard was elected
U.S. vice president under
Dwight D. Eisenhower.
Richard decided to run for
president in 1960. He lost the
election to John F. Kennedy.

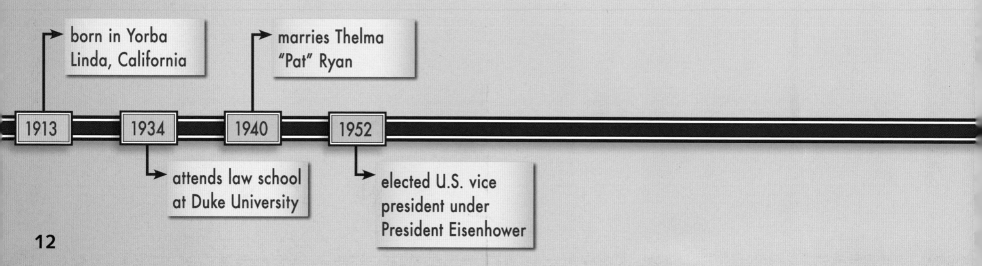

born in Yorba
Linda, California

marries Thelma
"Pat" Ryan

1913

1934

1940

1952

attends law school
at Duke University

elected U.S. vice
president under
President Eisenhower

Richard and Dwight D. Eisenhower

Richard went back to working as a lawyer. But he missed politics. Richard ran for governor of California in 1962 but lost the election. Richard decided to run for president again in 1968. This time, he won.

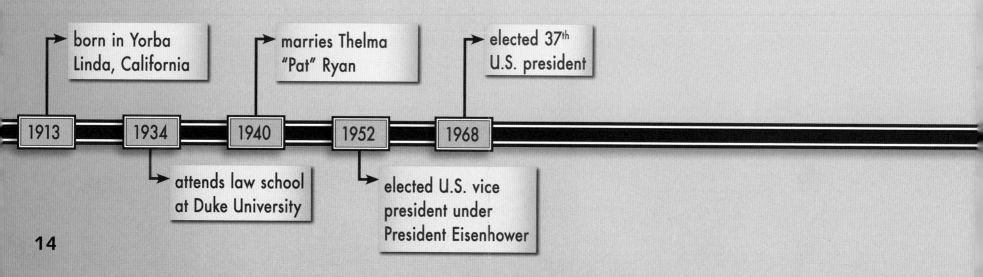

born in Yorba
Linda, California

marries Thelma
"Pat" Ryan

elected 37th
U.S. president

1913   1934   1940   1952   1968

attends law school
at Duke University

elected U.S. vice
president under
President Eisenhower

President Nixon

As president, Richard faced many challenges. One was the Vietnam War (1959–1975). Richard worked to end the war. In 1972, Richard was re-elected president.

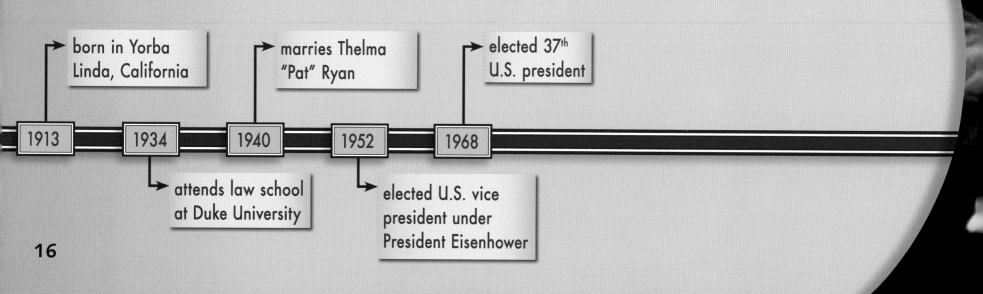

| 1913 | 1934 | 1940 | 1952 | 1968 |

- **1913** — born in Yorba Linda, California
- **1934** — attends law school at Duke University
- **1940** — marries Thelma "Pat" Ryan
- **1952** — elected U.S. vice president under President Eisenhower
- **1968** — elected 37th U.S. president

Richard visits U.S. troops in Vietnam in 1969.

Richard is best known for the Watergate scandal. The U.S. Congress wanted to remove Richard from office because of Watergate. He resigned as president on August 9, 1974.

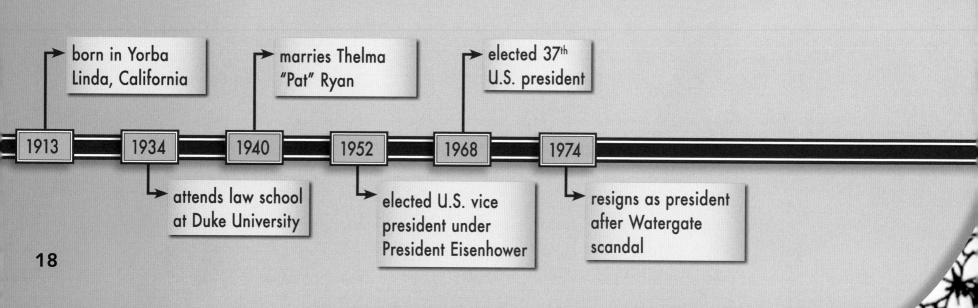

born in Yorba Linda, California

1913

marries Thelma "Pat" Ryan

1934

attends law school at Duke University

1940

1952

elected U.S. vice president under President Eisenhower

elected 37th U.S. president

1968

1974

resigns as president after Watergate scandal

19

After his presidency, Richard wrote books about politics. He died on April 22, 1994. Richard is remembered for pulling the United States out of the Vietnam War. He is the only president to resign from office.

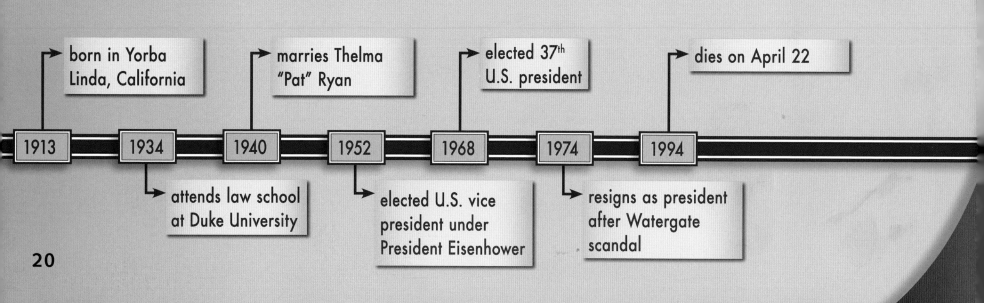

born in Yorba Linda, California

marries Thelma "Pat" Ryan

elected 37th U.S. president

dies on April 22

| 1913 | 1934 | 1940 | 1952 | 1968 | 1974 | 1994 |

attends law school at Duke University

elected U.S. vice president under President Eisenhower

resigns as president after Watergate scandal

Glossary

elect—to choose someone by voting

politics—the act of governing a city, state, or country

resign—to give up a job, position, or office

scandal—an action or event that angers a lot of people

senator—one of the 100 people that makes laws in the Senate

student body president—the highest-ranking member of the student body

U.S. House of Representatives—one of two houses in the U.S. Congress that makes laws

Vietnam War—the conflict from 1954 to 1975 between South Vietnam and North Vietnam

Read More

Britton, Tamara L. *Richard Nixon.* The United States Presidents. Edina, Minn.: ABDO, 2009.

Dell, Pamela. *Show Me the U.S. Presidency: My First Picture Encyclopedia.* My First Picture Encyclopedias. North Mankato, Minn.: Capstone Press, 2014.

Donaldson, Madeline. *Richard Nixon.* History Maker Bios. Minneapolis: Lerner Pub, 2008.

Internet Sites

FactHound offers a safe, fun way to find Internet sites related to this book. All of the sites on FactHound have been researched by our staff.

Here's all you do:

Visit *www.facthound.com*

Type in this code: 9781476596129

23

Critical Thinking Using the Common Core

1. Richard was a lawyer and later, the U.S. vice president under Dwight D. Eisenhower. How do you think these jobs helped Richard as president? (Integration of Knowledge and Ideas)

2. Look at the photo on page 15. What is Richard doing? What clues did you use in the photo and the text to help you answer this question? (Craft and Structure)

3. Richard resigned as U.S. president after people found out about the Watergate scandal. What does it mean to resign? What clues in the text help you figure out the meaning? (Key Ideas and Details)

Index

Word Count: 269
Grade: 1
Early-Intervention Level: 23